Jungle Animals

SLOTHS

By Rob Ryndak

Gareth Stevens
PUBLISHING

Please visit our website, www.garethstevens.com. For a free color catalog of all our high-quality books, call toll free 1-800-542-2595 or fax 1-877-542-2596.

Library of Congress Cataloging-in-Publication Data

Ryndak, Rob.
Sloths / by Rob Ryndak.
p. cm. — (Jungle animals)
Includes index.
ISBN 978-1-4824-1761-6 (pbk.)
ISBN 978-1-4824-1762-3 (6-pack)
ISBN 978-1-4824-1760-9 (library binding)
1. Sloths — Juvenile literature. I. Title.
QL737.E2 R96 2015
599.3–d23

First Edition

Published in 2015 by
Gareth Stevens Publishing
111 East 14th Street, Suite 349
New York, NY 10003

Editor: Ryan Nagelhout
Designer: Katelyn E. Reynolds

Photo credits: Cover, pp. 1, 15 worldswildlifewonders/Shutterstock.com; p. 5 Nacho Such/Shutterstock.com; p. 7 Vilainecrevette/Shutterstock.com; pp. 9, 13 Kjersti Joergensen/Shutterstock.com; p. 11 Suzi Eszterhas/Minden Pictures/Getty Images; p. 17 Bill Hatcher/National Geographic/Getty Images; pp. 19, 23, 24 (leaves) Joost van Uffelen/Shutterstock.com; pp. 21, 24 (toes) Eric Isselee/Shutterstock.com.

Printed in the United States of America

CPSIA compliance information: Batch #CW15GS: For further information contact Gareth Stevens, New York, New York at 1-800-542-2595.

Contents

Sloths are
very slow animals.

They sleep a lot.

They live in trees.

Even their babies
are born in trees!

They are very good at climbing.

Their back legs are
very weak.
They can't walk
on land.

They are very good at swimming!

They eat leaves and fruit.

Some have two toes.

Others have three toes.

Words to Know

leaves

toes

Index